C. Fenn
4-21-84

BILLIE BEETHOVEN

By the same author

HIS & HERS

BILLIE BEETHOVEN

POEMS BY BILLIE BARBARA MASTEN

SUNFLOWER INK
Palo Colorado Canyon
Carmel, Calif. 93923

ACKNOWLEDGMENTS

These poems would not have been possible without the assistance of Jeanne MacGregor and Melinda Douglas. They not only lent me their heads and hands but also gave me the support I needed to keep going on this project.

Particular thanks to my mother Minnie Grace Glover Bolton for stroking my rebelliousness and to Ric Masten for showing me how to move on it . . . and to all the people who's heads I have slept with.

The book was produced by CLACK & NICHOLS, A PARTNERSHIP, 403 North Texas, Odessa, Texas. 79761

(paperback) 9 8 7 6 5 4 3 2 1

Library of Congress Catalogue Card No. 83-50940

ISBN 0-931104-13-0

TABLE OF CONTENTS

For Jerri, April, Stuart and Ellen

INTRODUCTION

"I accept the Universe!" wrote Transcendentalist, Margaret Fuller. Thomas Carlisle replied . . . "she'd better."

"But she didn't have to accept her situation," I can hear Billie Barbara Masten saying, defying her own traditional religious training. In her art as in her poetry, Billie approaches an understanding of the depth of the injustice done to her and to the other women throughout history.

Billie Barbara speaks for women who came together in the late nineteen sixties and early nineteen seventies. I was one of those women, and with the help of my Sisters I realized that I didn't have to accept the Universe as it had been presented to me: as Male, as Authority. Now I could begin to be able to see to what extent disadvantage had shaped me.

Words became newly important. The meanings had been obscured and twisted by misnomers and mistaken notions, distorting poetry, philosophy, history, psychology, religion. Language corrupted, corrupts thought. Billie Barbara Masten is Feminism expressing *Herself:* her past confusion, her struggle to redefine who she is, to stop feeling "pushed around." Since the "pushing around" has been structured with men on top for at least five thousand years, with men and women acting as if sex and marriage are power relationships, it is not surprising that we are not sure what we are to do now. Women are talking for themselves—expression.

"I feel so good about my changes, to be able to use what I have. As I become more and more human I *need* to translate my feelings into words."

Billie Barbara found she had been an artist and a

poet hiding herself in a closet labeled "housewife", waiting for twenty years to come out.

Billie's poetry is fiercely personal, basic, "intense", they call it. I call it vibrant. Her first book, *The Beast And The Bad Girl,* was woman-little-girl bravado. "I wrote it because I had to," says Billie Barbara, all guts and struggle. Women who were angry and hurt felt an instant identification. Billie's accumulated feelings ranged, like Sylvia Plath's or Anne Sexton's, through rage/pain/desperation, trapped in past conditioning, tormented in the present, yet excited by her future. Billie broke through her conflict, enticed by her growing awareness of her own potential. "I will speak for myself!"

Billie speaks for herself now with the rough edges worn away, polished, thoughtful, reflective: Billie with Style. *Billie Beethoven* explores old feelings of guilt and shame through her unconscious. "I want to surface the unknown that's knowable. A part of me still wants to blame and to hate, but I know how much I need other people now."

Billie Beethoven is written for sharing. Why don't we know more about Beethoven's mother? Why have so few women expressed themselves in lasting ways? Have we been so ignored?

While we ponder that question we can experience a woman's personal poetic statement here and now, in print. "The greatest influence in the world is "word power", says Billie Barbara. She claims her power and the rest of us who love words know what she means. This second Ms. Masten (Mrs. Ric is gone), reminds us that caring and sharing for both men and women are our only hopes. What we are working for is the time when there will be no monopoly on "being" or "doing" and when there will be enough love to go around.

Roberta Richards
Phoenix, Arizona

1.

OWNING THE BEAST AND THE BAD GIRL

OWNING the BEAST And The BAD GIRL *came out of sharing a program with Ric about our relationship.*

These poems are my feelings leading up to a break in that relationship and the most remarkable change in my life.

I had attended a class at Starr King School for the Ministry. Margaret Williams and Til Evans, our leaders, convinced me that journal keeping was like a string on my memory. It reminded me of the dream logging I had done. If I could recall just a little, I could pull back alot. Then Ric said if I didn't want to be news reporting—writing something like Ric hurt me today, then I must tell how it feels to hurt and make it a poem.

Writing helps me recollect what I already know. I had kept my journal in chaos and madness, the sweet madness of creation, hoping for the morning star. Going back over these strange writings I was able to pull back The BEAST and the BAD GIRL.

(To give value to my efforts is creative).

Learning to own my feelings I found crazy-making anger, hidden violence and hostility. I use dream logging, journal keeping and wood carving to reach these raw sources of energy. I hope to own the energy of self-hate and discounting. The devaluation of myself is a huge loss of power, all the kick-me and nail-me-up attitudes so unproductive and learned so well.

What can I do instead of what did I do? In the latter of those two phrases I already assume guilt, even before proven guilty. All these things I've used to make myself wooden.

The wood carvings are another way for me to see me. All part of my religious evolution. I have always expressed myself some through crafts, sewing, gardening, cooking, etc. I now wish to take anger, the volcanos and violent storms, and release that earth shaking power and transform that vitality into something society will accept.

I gave myself permission to do this with this little phrase ANYTHING WORTH DOING IS WORTH DOING POORLY.

Others can teach me how they do it. Ultimately I must take the first step.

TO RIC

And he stood solid
Letting the sharp word edges
Bounce off
Fall away—
Until we could come together again
And touch.

MANY COLORS

Before I got there
Like being over forty,
The dry brown California hills
Seemed old and ugly.

Up close
            a miner in my forties
I worked those hills for gold.
Found Joseph's coat,
A rainbow,
The 4th of July exploding,
Sunsets and much new
                growing.

ALMOST EMPTY-NESTED

Swimming underwater
My eyes brown fish, pond-bound
Distorting wearing an old prescription.
My main interest—the family
Going out of focus, the picture blurs
Darkness comes down on me like sunglasses
And stains the sun.

My husband's breath turns sour,
My kiss is bitter lipped.

Where have I hidden my picture?
The one of me, alone.
Put away so carefully—I can't find it
Along with my self-confidence.

I weep, strangely sad.
I feel tragic.
A trapped animal, chained, howling here, mad,
I scream sometimes with and
Sometimes without a voice.

DREAM No. 1

And I beheld the beasts and demons.
The beasts that are and are not and yet are
And I would not own them.

I was walking just a passerby out of the night,
When this beast rose in the dark,
A dog actually. He bit me
In all the excitement.
And our mutual fright,
Me the center of the universe
Caught in a dog's bite.
Hampered like clothes waiting for laundry,
A kite caught in a tree,
A cow waiting for slaughter,
Speak Jesus speak. Turn this stone,
Speak. Set me free.

I was robed in a Jane Eyre,
Wuthering Height's gown.

It was a waiting dress.

WAIT YOUR TURN

And I have waited,
I waited to grow up—use lipstick,
To be kissed, to wear a bra, for my prince
To come, to vote.
I waited for some man to ask me to marry him
And have children.
I waited in lines for stamps and groceries,
In lobbies for movies,
In parked cars for children at lessons,
For airplanes to come bringing you in,
For airplanes to go taking you out.
I waited for the roast to get done, the jello
To set, the light to turn green.
Waiting to move on, to go away on vacations
To go back home—the children grew up
And my hair has turned gray.
And I have waited
For you to ask me to speak
For myself.
Hey! It's my turn. I will speak for myself.

IN OUR HOUSE

In our house Ric's old Underwood sits silent
On the end of our ancient olivewood table.

John Lennon screams, "Weelll"
On our record player.

Jerri is drawing a picture of our pepper mill
April sleeps and dreams in her room.

Ellen thinks of washing her hair
          But there is no shampoo.

Stuart rode off on his motorcycle to visit
          Our neighbors the Pughs.

Ric is away in Boston with Sarah
          And Norman working.

While I sit in bed waiting.
          Lonely already

Thinking, "Is this all there is?"

ONLY THE NOW

I can't go with you
After all there are the kids.
It was you, you were the one
Who always said;
"Only the now
That's all there is."
And when I did go along
I was the old shoe
Comfortable forgotten
You were the closed door—

The elevator always somewhere else
On another floor.

A WOMAN'S PLACE

Why do I long for another place
When I have my place.
This place where I can walk a country road
With my dogs running up ahead,
Tune in on a bird's song,
Hear insect-rattle noises,
See sky blues,
Clouds, trees, bushes,
Flower yellows.
Why do I long for another place
When I have this place, my place,
A woman's place?

NO SLEEP

In the night quiet
With only the freezer machine noise
I think of the bad things
That drive sleep away.
Every inch of me screams tired.
It's as if I purposely think way back to
Stressful things.
I let them surface
Just enough to keep me
On the edge of sleep.

HER BRIEF LIFE

Once I watched a tiny thirsty butterfly
Drink in her brief life.
And out there in the sun for a single moment
I bathed in beauty.
Her's and mine
And thought about death.

ONE MORNING

Seeing only stones in my path,
Weeds in my garden,
Dirty hand prints on the window glass
And too many dirty dishes in the
Kitchen sink.
I wonder why
I get up—dress myself—cook and eat.
I hate it here, standing at the sink.
I try thinking of this as my discipline
Like karate, or a ballet lesson.
I recite verses.
I try to become the dishes, the water, the soap.
I think how glad I am that I have hands.
Today I just stand here.
Tears blinding me from those soapy things.
I feel chained to the sink,
Chained to the house.

MAGNET

I run away from the house
Until I can't see it.
I hurry up, fast like something's
After me.
Up the hill, behind the house,
Until I'm nothing but a heart beat.
I lie down on the ground.
I feel Indian. My ancient sisters
Are calling me back in time,
To do sun worship.
I do, just for an instant,
Then I can feel the pull of my duties
Drawing me back
To the house, to the children, the trees.

OUT OF EASE

My eyes are blind.
My ears are stones.
The beasts are after me. Uneasy.
I drive the car into town.
'Fraid to look into the back seat,
Because I know that she-devil is
Riding there.

I start spending long hours
Cutting eyes, photographed and printed
From magazines.
I fill my room with these eyes,
Pasting them everywhere, on boxes,
My dresser. I paint a giant eye
On my window.

She peers down
Watching me from everywhere.
I noticed I've neglected my toenails.
They grow long and sharp.

And I let the beast take possession
Of my mouth, my hands,
Awful sounds,
Slaps, filth,
Burning accusations,
Hurt, blame, sores, wounds,
And much dis-ease.

THE BAD GIRL

I was recognized.
She recognized me.
Our man-hate oozed out—poison.

At first we were joined, clinging, kissing,
Loud.
Then she started drinking.
I went out—still on my feet.
She moved, ran naked,
Screamed and cursed.
I was dead!
Drunk!

That was she,
Jezebel.
See how she paints her eyes.
Throw her down for the dogs to eat,
Cast her out,
She's Eve.

I'm my Daddy's good little girl.
The bad girl,
That's she.
She couldn't possibly be   me.

DREAM NO. II

One night as the moon watched—
Silent, at the window.
I dreamed I came upon a cow,
Grazing in the field upon a mountain side,
Encircled by a fence.
As I looked close she changed
Before me, into another kind of beast.
One I had never seen before.
I took her into my bed to lie with her
She would have kicked me to death
But as I looked into her eyes
They rolled white—

I knew, named and owned her.
She was my fear.

NO ONE EVER TOLD ME

No one told me my need to die
Would be as great as my need to live,
That beauty fades,
That I would look right at and not see,
Listen, but not hear,
That in anger at my children,
So lovable, so darling,
I would curl my fist
And wish to strike them down.
No one told me that I would hit my husband,
That he would hit back,
"Men never hit women,"
My daddy always said.
No one told me that the mind,
            emotions can distort,
Change everything,
That a primal beast can live with a
Heavenly angel.
That I, Mary, Mother of God, and I,
Medea would dwell side by side
In this one woman.

DON'T YOU KNOW ME

Right about here ol' Eric Berne
Came along and whispered in my ear.
I shouted to every traveler on the road,
"Don't you know me?"
"Who are you?" they asked;
"Why, I'm the working man's daughter.
I'm my daddy's good little girl."

"Make me laugh, Daddy"
And he would, he would
It felt so good, so good
Sometimes I laughed until I cried.

NO BLAME

My house was dark.
Alone, I ran out of dreams,
Fell off the mountain,
Flew away over cities,
Had an affair.
The quartered moon poker-red,
Burned into the darker depths,
Beyond the blame.

On this side of sleep
I lie down on my fuzzy white coat.
Reading Castaneda's words
Until the fog filling the canyon looks green.
If it were water
I could swim to another place.
I need to see things differently.
I can't be you, Mama,
Drowning in the berry patch
In the middle years.
All those years hiding in the guest room
While your quiet war cut away,
Raw and bleeding,
My strength leaving me
I dream of dying,
But my gardens are lush and green.

Something is dying.
Let me out!

HAPPY BIRTHDAY

I was born on the twenty-second of July
To Minnie Grace Glover
And William Mattison Bolton.
They called me Billie, long before I was born.
According to my birth story
Mama Minnie baked a birthday cake
For Daddy Bill
Before she went to the San Bernardino
County Hospital
To give birth to little Bill.

I came out Barbara.
Happy Birthday for she's a jolly good fellow.

No one called me Barbara
Until I insisted on it.
I was seven and in the second grade.
I loved my daddy.
I wanted to please him so much,
Now at forty I still feel a little bit sad.
"But I'm a woman now," I said,
"A woman in full bloom."
I was Billie a little bit sad.
I was Barbara a woman in full bloom.
So I named myself Billie Barbara
And the healing began.

I'm in Death Valley—it's the
Middle of the school year.
Christmas—Joy to the World!
I dream I'm driving but keep
Falling asleep at the wheel.
This is the first time I've been away
So long from you, Mama, in all my forty years
Our bed is too crowded
For you to sleep between us, Ric says.
"Let go of me," I scream
And hold on to her tighter
Of course my mama and I finally
Did get divorced.

LOOKING FOR DADDY

In the beginning, determined
Like Ruth of the Bible
To give up mama's God
I traveled to foreign states
With my husband.
Lodged in motels
Where my husband lodged.

We moved around, changed positions,
Argued, fought, differed in opinion
Loved each other an awful lot.

But this morning I feel tired, lonely,
A little bit sad,
Scared sister to Orpah
I return looking for Daddy,
Longing to tell him
I'll come home.
I'll be nice
I'm still your good little girl.

I'm homesick for mama
I want safety, her care,
To be taken into the warmth,
The comfort,
Of their big, overpowering, unmoveable bed.

I call her on the phone.
She's slipping, losing out, going backward.

Spends a lot of time in the past,
In her head.
And my Daddy, O God
My very own Daddy

Daddy, Daddy
I just realized
You Are Dead.

LOT'S WIFE

After twenty years of marriage
I remember Lot's wife,
"Looking back from behind him,"
Loveless and bitter,
Left,
Refusing to move on,
A piller of salt,
Alone.

COLOR ME BLUE

This morning
My back hurts.
Under my brown eyes
There are bags.
My skin wrinkles and sags.
There is no sun,
The buildings are cold gray stones.
Last night I dreamed of dying.
Color me blue
I'm forty-two.

JULY 4TH, AGE 43

I keep my journal in chaos
And like my dreams
I go back over these words, symbols
Making sense and order,
Giving meaning.

I will create my world.
I will own my feelings.
I will take control of my own life
Mama and Daddy.

I HEAR

In the morning
Before the dawn
Thoughts come crashing down,
Holding me under—
Drowning me—
Suddenly from the depths
Of that dark seabed
I hear
And my mind
Comes floating up—
Reaching out—
Clinging—
To a bird's morning song,
Healing notes—
Singing—I arise.

I SEE

Looking back at my life
I remember—
How I bit,
        screamed,
        hit,
        cried,
Shaking the bed—
Shaking the man—
Shaking the child—
Shaking the woman, me awake—
I'm fighting hard to keep my eyes
Open
Now that I've finally started to see.

I AM

I go down into the dark tunnel
Where my dream part is.
I am not afraid,
Because all that power and ability is mine.
I make big—fly—burn—feel pleasure
Feel fear.

How strong I am.
I shrink, enlarge, bend,
Color, paint, embroider.
Hear slogans. See ghosts.
Someone calls my name.
I grow small and disappear.
I run partly covered, naked, in my underwear.
I am a buffalo, two elephants,
A mythical bird.

I climb tilting structures . . . endless . . .
Bake a magic cake.
Dig through tunnels of impossible dirt
Out to glorious light.
I am a curving road, beautiful ladies,
Warm soothing water, a song,
A wrinkled baby, hair in a mirror with no face,
Wild hair, to cut and groom,
Black widow spider, all mothers,
Front and back,
The eye and now the ear.

I am well/sick, death/life,

A script, a novel, stories.
I am here.
I am now.
I am a field of glittering, sparkling stars
Of night,
Three men in black,
Two cars,
I AM
BILLIE BARBARA.

LETTING GO

The wind blows
The tree moves—letting go
Old leaves for new

2.

NOTES THROWN FROM A PASSING CAR

NOTES THROWN FROM A PASSING CAR
are poems about particular events in different states. We were at the U.N. when vegetarianism was going to feed the world.

NEW YORK

At the U.N. we talked about world hunger,
Ate vegetarian,
Looked at Chinese ivory carved.
A rug of the Wall of China hung on the wall.

The Vienna Boy's Choir in navy blue
With cameras in place of crucifixes
Sang a hymn to a rock from the moon
In a case lighted like a jewel.

I circled dizzily in Liberty's head.
Viewed the outside of Ellis Island.
Got to see inside in "Godfather, II".

I got mad about something, ran out
Onto the street of N.Y., N.Y.
Stepped into something left by a dog
But from previously sitting in some
Knew that dog stuff can wash off
If we live through this drought.

KEYS TO THE CITY

And God said, I will set
My bow in the clouds for a sign.

Stopped at a red light
My first time in New York City
A man approached my side of the car.
He had one hand hidden in his pocket
I'd been warned before to lock my door.

His eyes caught mine
And they fastened.
I rolled down my window just one inch.
He slipped them in on tiny pieces of paper
Rainbows
For you wonderful people from California
That's all he said.

FT. LAUDERDALE, FLORIDA

One of the hardest things about being on-the-road is leaving people. Getting to know and love them, then having to say goodbye knowing we might not meet again. I had just decided I was going to not feel when I met Chandra Ice.

Inside the Green House State
I found her like a plant growing in the dark.
Her white spidery stems
So thin and fragile they looked too long
For her pretty sixteen year old face.
She wrote her first poems that week.
One to her father was extraordinary.
It was hard for her to walk, to breathe.
I carried her, held her up.
I was free from the pain of not caring
But I did not escape.

"My ability to love makes me vulnerable;
Vulnerability is also my power."
Margaret Williams Braxton

Faces, names I won't remember
But spirits rise.
Today's horoscope reads
"Don't over react to criticism."
Anger, it covers my fear.
I want my mama.
I buy new clothes
Navy blue shoes help.
I visit the art museum.
A castle's view and the wind's roar
Pulls me up
Out of the dark hole.
Peruvian artifacts like
Deformities become my sin.
Guilt encased in stone
Brought down over hundreds of years.
Bent over under this load
I struggle hard to stand.

DALLAS COUNTY JAIL, TEXAS

The man in the glass box
Checks out her ID as
She explains about me.
He nods and the green metal gates
Open like jaws.
We move in.

The door just ahead opens
And we walk through.
The door closes
And I can hear it lock.
I am locked in.

She has keys for the next two doors
Which must be left locked behind us
Even the elevator has green metal gates
That must be unlocked
And left locked.
The elevator goes up.
Doors open.
Doors close.
Metal slams against metal.
Iron locks iron.
Metal on metal turning.
Metal opening metal.
Metal slamming metal.
Metal locking metal.
Metal locking me in.

I dream I'm on the beach

The ocean waves are rising around me.
I'm in an open car
Driving on the rims
Screaming metal.
Down a steep hill
Down a long hall
Into a room.

Thirty-five women and I.
Oceans of doors locking us in
On the tenth floor
In the Dallas County Jail
For three hours.

I did what I could
To make it a picnic.

READING (pronounced Redding) Penna.

County Home for the Aging
Christmas Eve, it's afternoon.

How could you kiss
Fold on fold
Crazy old crones
Arms and legs bags of bones
Screams from holes no teeth.

Too much skin
Too much smell of urine.

My eyes fill, spill
But I dance I sing
The wisdom of the fool
'Till nearly everyone laughs or smiles
A few even sing.

My Daddy, my Mama,
My Grandpa, my Great Aunt Sadie
My self,
One day sitting there.

3.

THE BIBLE REVISITED

THE BIBLE REVISITED.
When I was a young Bible student, Ruth Williams was the first teacher who explained that words are symbols and until we have experiences to give meaning to them that's all they are. We make the Word come to life.

THE SAME OLD BOAT

And the rain fell forty days
And forty nights
And the waters prevailed
And the ark floated upon the face
Of the woman

She rose up—a sudden flood out of our audience.
A tidal wave of her suffering swept over us
Left behind horror pictures of self-inflicted wounds
And needless guilts.

After the heavy rain,
Unlike Noah's dove
Set free,
She'd found no dry ground on which to rest
Saw nothing new in all we'd said
Not a single green twig, no olive leaf.

She left in the same old hopeless boat
She'd seen no signs for wonder
Nor had she heard any promise
about a rainbow.

GENESIS I

They were a pair of giants
King Kong and his queen,
Daddy and Mama.

It was no small outpouring of seed.
But Eros meeting Eros face to face
Fire upon fire
A connection, dynamism, tension,
Lightning flashed, thunder roared.
Monsoon rained down fire
Till all the wind of the world
Was warm.

They were at beginnings—creation, Genesis
They were as one.
Love, the glue of the world,
Held them.

A tiny ovum found courage
Shot in an arc from her safety
An island rose in his sea
Such flashings, zappings,
The electric hot wire.

It was an event.
It was an energy event.
It was the beginning of me.
Here my struggle with gravity began.

REVOLUTION THROUGH LANGUAGE
ALTERED STATES

A young man asked me
Where was God in all my growth
What part had He played?!?

Gray steel rain cuts the sky
The arm with the hammer
Attacks the house.
Her moans break me loose from dreams
Beside me he sleeps.
I am alone with my fear
I want to go back to sleep
But I am awake now.
Like Jacob with the unknown man
"I wrestle 'till dawn"
With my old ways of thinking, old worn out
Words that teach sexism, racism
Exclude me.
Pinned down desperate for new
Expressions to tell in everyday language
How I feel
What I value
And about the person I wish to become
I release rage into this revolution.
Jacob won his fight
But the angel wounded his hip
Pinched his sciatic muscle
'till he limped.

Wound me faithfully
I must evolve.

GUILT

"I must forgive the past"

Jean Carter Stapleton

And God said speak to the rock
But like Moses I struck. I slapped your face
When a few words spoken
Would have brought forth the water—
The tears from your eyes.

For his act his God within
Would not forgive.
He never entered the Promised Land.
I was forty before I got
To this place
Where I can forgive myself
        Happy Beulah Land
        Oh Canaan Fair.

Guilt—psychological—hangs on—won't let go
                makes me sick
    existential   pulls me to change.

Owning My Male Parts

In a dream
Like Pharaoh's daughter
Bathing in the Nile
I find unexpected
In my egg-shaped basket
Evolution.

An ovum becomes a tiny baby
A boy
A hero person
A savior
A Jesus King.

In the thick rushes
On the edge of dreams flowing
Latent with a thousand sister eyes
I keep the watch
I drink the water
It sustains my life.

The strong healthy baby
Grows up in my dreams
I am the protector, the savior.
I am the carrier of my life
I, am the Prince.

RELIGION—THE INGATHERING

The wind sister
Chants her morning song.
Combing tangles from my mind
She plaits my scattered selves
Into a single braid. ooommmmmmmmmm

A SISTER

I was down
Thinking in hospitals
Of Uncle Bud dying
When the wind pulled me up by the hair.

She breathed into the cracks
Pushed against the pain
Hovered out there with ghosts—
Dead friends Bonnie, Josh, Helen.

She sent the sound of many feet
Running down the hall
Shook and stirred my house
Til I heard the bells
On the front porch.

When I dance, I think like summer storms,
Sudden flashings, thunder rolling,
earth shaking thoughts.

But like dreams so often when I wake,
When the music stops they are gone.

When I dance I go inside my body,
I can see—hear inside my ears.
I move in a sound and beat world of harp and oboe.
I have reached the land of no more sorrow.
I have found the place of no more tears.

I get into bed
My Sweet Lord spins round on the record player.
I sit there
Trying to get my feet into the lotus position.
Out the window
Now playing in marvelous technicolor
"The Sunset Sky".

Jane Eyre floats in and out
On the balmy summer's air.
Sweet rivers of song
Roll over me.
In time I get up, dance.
I feel whole in my body.
I move with a new sense of worth-ship.

I dance with a God called Joy!

I'm found, healed
In a state of grace.
I start to move, circle like a spoon
Stirring within the safety
The limits of this new found cup.
5-7-10 years sacred numbers
Found in *Passages*.
Then the cup starts to leak, breaks in two.
I struggle again with dreams, reality,
My male and female parts,
Time for myself and service to others.
I struggle with language,
Conditioning, speaking out,
Defining my values,
Becoming non-violent,
Transforming hate.

I wonder if the woman's movement
Will be evolution or just
Another revolving door.

4.

BILLIE BEETHOVEN

BILLIE BEETHOVEN is dedicated to things hardly ever mentioned or talked about out loud, like Beethoven's mother. I don't even know her name. Do you?

Hey, Ms. Beethoven, why can't you be like all the other Steppford wives?

I will leave my pile of shells. My handprint on the cave wall. My face in the wood. My footprint in stone for my great grandchildren, and maybe yours.

"They got a name for the winners of this world. I want a name even when I lose." Steeley Dan.

The sad thing about this quote is, some of us want identity so badly we will take the names crazy, drunk, suicide, even murderer rather than get no recognition at all.

Hello, my name is Billie and I am an alcoholic.

GET ME A HORSE

I arrive at the party befuddled
I'm late a little—drunk
I don't understand their talk
Like a foreign language.
I feel left out
Different than they.
I don't think they like me.
I haven't done anything-yet.
They don't even know me.
I'm Lady Godiva
Get me a horse
I need attention
I'm suffering
Can't you see
I'm afraid.
So I drink some more.
I think I'm cute, playful.
To my children I'm an embarrassment.
To the others
Just an old woman
Pulling on a young man's hair.

APPROPRIATE BEHAVIOR

It was a funeral.
A remembrance.
I'd already had a few
The pain killers only drugged me
Separated me like divorce.
Afraid of death and dying
I wanted to be close.
But I wouldn't take it
From the young friendly at first.
The others ignored me.
They did't even stare
When I talked loud
Like mother on the telephone.
When I pushed and shoved people like Daddy
I did it with vulgar, angry words.
Alone in the crowd
I closed my eyes and ears to all I'd learned
Gave up the ghosts
Laid down with the corpse
And drowned in the booze.

My eyes—stubborn alcoholics
Won't leave the ground.
My memory benumbed by the drinks
Runs away and disappears.
In the dark a beast screams.
I run to the roof.
The lights flood.
The electric face appears
Illuminating colors like an old Bible
Saying, I love you.
I have always loved you.
And I shall always love you, like God.
Repeating what I'd already said.
Then the vapors of booze rise
I'm too far back in the fog to believe,
To trust.
I won't give up the hurt.
Hate me, let your eyes run from me in disgust.
How else can I validate my feelings
Of guilt and despair?
Why else would I keep on running?
My heart ticking with this bomb
Like the fox in the night screaming for love.
I am in the dark falling down
Blind and drunk.

Vacant lots
Deserts thirsty for green
My eyes restless runners like old city birds
Search the streets even the gutters
For crumbs. The answers
                    the treasures
                    the gold
Thrown out along the way by others.

Feet burning, soul wearing thin
Not old not young I lie down
Refusing to die.
In the dark I sleep.

I wake up
Remembering my dreams.
I find treasures,
Parts of me I'd thrown out,
Gold I'd disowned.

THE ADVERSARY

"No one can put you down unless you give them permission" *Eleanor Roosevelt*

The trees black
The road black
The moon hides.
It's Heathcliff's sky.
I walk silhouetted

Sudden as guilt
A tiger leaps.
He bites my arm
But lands on my nurturing mother's back.
She almost died.

The unknown man
Welding a great "Psycho" knife
Cuts out the teeth.
And the T.V. director escapes
From my arm.
The wound comes together and heals.
The teeth are the exact
Color and shape of my own.

In my house
Tiger's teeth wait

BEAST DREAM NO. III

"How can we be responsible for what we won't acknowledge?" *Rollo May*

Response—ability

I dreamed her up
The old she-beast
Looked kind of like a bat
Except she had lazer beam eyes
Burning gold holes into the black.

She woke me in such fright
I noticed even our friend Rodger
Down in the guest room
Kept his lights on all through the night.

She reappeared the next night
Split herself into
A triad of heads on one bat.

Next morning Rodger asked me
If I'd named what I saw
I named them,
SELF HATE, BLIND RAGE and BLAME.
Since then she hasn't bothered to come
Back into my dreams.

BEAST DREAM NO. V

I am in my living room
Looking out the picture window.
A prehistoric bird circles
With a garbage disposal mouth.

The old she-beast hideous
With man-eating teeth
Wants to eat up my tree.
But the needles and trunk
Are sharp and thick
Hard to swallow.
The man in the shadows
Hands me a gun, "Kill her."
"No, I don't believe in killing."

Later down in the kitchen
I carve her with my steely knife.
I cut her out of the wood of my life.
A woman's head with fangs,
A female dracula,
Beauty's beast,
Old as religion.

I mean to burn her
Throw her into the fire
Be rid of her.

I never will
You have to own dragons to fly.

LETTING MY DEAD DAD REST

When Daddy died
I didn't cry.
I went numb instead.

After reading Castaneda
Daddy appeared in my dream, a coyote,
Changed into a cloud,
Blew away and disappeared.

Bigger than real life
And capable of magic,
Able to dance more than a two-step,
He can do whatever I like.
I own and control my own past.
Even so I won't let go.

The summer three years later,
I lay on the floor out of my self and
Watched a forty year old woman
Throw a two year old's fit.
How could you leave me?
I hate you for leaving me.
I was your good little girl.

Hypnagogic: beyond small errors

Later in a dream
I saw a house he'd built
Yet not made with his hand.
He was in the garden working.

Young, handsome, a full head of hair,
        without spot or blemish,
Beautifully dressed, no lint.

At the window a grown-up woman now,
I stand beside my man.
Daddy sees us, smiles and waves his hand.

I wake up crying.

THE WEANING

after reading Kierkegaard

Looking at pavement
All my life.
Every step taken
To avoid the crack.
All that summer
Mama's needs were so great
I almost fell in, got sick all over again.

Mother, may I
Take one giant step forward on my own
Without three baby steps back?
Yes, daughter, you may.
She withdrew her breast.
When I started to get comfortable,
Relaxed with this,
She reversed the game
Asking me for my permission to do things.

Mama, please take your giant step,
Stand on your own.
It's okay to be your own mother I said
And withdrew my breast.

She heard me four years later after
Daddy died.

Happy is the daughter

Who gives birth to her mother.
Happier still is the daughter whose mother
Gives birth to her mother
No matter how far along in life she is.

FEELING MY AGE

He slowed down his car.
Coming up from behind
After seeing my face
He called as he stepped on the gas,
"You've still got a fine lookin' ass."

I WISH MY MOTHER COULD APPROVE MY SUCCESS

A woman aged 63 said,
My mother aged 91
Is strong as a bear,
Sharp as a pin.
Why each morning
Over the phone
She can still
Tie a ribbon in my hair.

A DAUGHTER

Relief welled in tiny streams
At the corners of her eyes.
Each time I could see what she said.

She said, "Mountains wear faces".
I said, "Mountains are faces-mouths open,
Pouring out rivers of blue sky".

Our power arched a rainbow over
The word flood and healed us.

She broke open my flesh
And flew out of my side
But left me whole.

A BUD

Sitting in the car.
Waiting for Ric.
Caged, closed up tight,
I start to write.
I feel envious, jealous of others,
Poets, artists, photographers,
Rollo May, Barbara Walters,
Clint Eastwood.

I look at the windshield.
Rain maps the glass,
Clear upon clear.

A woman in a wheel chair
With no umbrella rolls past.
A tree twists and turns.
Knocked about but not down.
They are, at least, a part of the dance.
Each blow of the wind parts the leaves
And I must cut my hair.

Seaweed rolfed by the current
Returns with the current
To do it all over again.
Why do I want to do it?
Write, expose myself.
Clark Mustakus said it,
"Each time you open
You never close back
Quite as tight as before."

And I dreamed from of my mouth
Frozen squares and triangles fell.

Outside chaos, madness dances in the leaves.
I do not hear its voice
Nor do I feel its torment.
Inside, four-squared, secure,
Protected, safe.

(chant) A fly climbs up the windowpane.
A boy sits reading.
A page turns.
The clock ticks.
The watch on my arm ticks.
A girl studies.
I cannot see her brain.

On the outer edges of this near silence
A bird cries, an airplane passes.
The poet's voice is reading down below.
I am the poet's wife
No longer waiting.
I am busy keeping myself alive
Freezing this picture onto this page.

In the summer of '77, age 44
I began to see her brain.
I gave myself permission to be smart.
I not only read Kierkegaard
I understood him.
I also started figuring out my own Income Tax!

IF ONLY I'D

After reading Adrienne Rich
I'm filled with fear and trembling
And a sense of dread.
I write too
On bits of toilet tissue
And kleenex.
I keep these pieces
Like the Xmas puzzle
In a box under the bed
Waiting.

Why am I waiting?
The kids are grown.
The bed is made.
Dishes done.

It's time
To work the pieces into something whole
Something to share
Before it's all been said
And everyone's gone home.

I want to try new things,
But guilt about the old duties left undone
Hangs on to my hand like a scared child.

Demons still wait
Steal my time
Dishes, beds, dust, feelings.

I worry about Ric,
The children grown now,
My ageing mother
Whether they're happy or sad.
I wish I could make them always happy.
I know no one can make me happy.
But I worry.
Worrying like this I will lose the day.

DAY DREAM

Look down mountains
Through the thick sweet pinks blooming.
The ocean is gold with sun-spangles.
I am in the orchard attending the saints.
I squat watering.
Tiny black deer flies
Try again and again to enter my eyes.
I tuck my head down under an arm, wing-like
A creature new-carved from dreams,
Part woman, part bird,
Yet old as totems, rests here.
I stir, an Indian Princess come to life,
Put a feather blue-black into my hair.
Natural, serene, Uooo, I like it here
The bright morning solitude, the quiet house
Somewhere between earth and sky.
Able to see and dream.

I notice moon-shaped seed pods all hairy
Clinging with new hope to my sweater.
Like them I too expect transformation—
Change to release new forms more life!

PALO COLORADO

A delicious aloneness.
The sun slipped out of her shape.
Cool, gray evening.

Before Christ came John.
A wild man
Wearing animal skins,
Eating insects and honey,
Paving the way,
Making the road for change.

THE GLASS SLIPPER

All that summer
When I swam
I was an otter.
"But do you remember your shoes?"
He asked
To change and to remember how—

FOLKLORE

There are wee people, trolls
One leaps.
Once more a demon of possibility
Rides on me piggy back

When I own my horns and fangs,
Beast and bad girl
My songs are fiercely real.
I sing
Stunned with wonder.
Astonishment *is* a source of longevity.

CELEBRATION

An orchestra swooping.
Tornados of sound
Lift me like birds.

It's high noon.
Billie in the field with demons.
But this time
I am illuminating myself.
Van Gogh is painting.
The green corn is waving
The sun.

Birds are flying up
Bird after bird
And for a single moment
I
Hang suspended
                                        somewhere
Between earth and sky.
Nailed to the cross.
Rising again.